MALA
OF THE
HEART

More praise for *Mala of the Heart*

"*Mala of the Heart* is an inspirational convergence of great saints, prophets, and poets who have walked the earth before us. It is a well-balanced anthology that reinspires us to remember the Source in whatever name or form that may take for us. The poems act like ancient aphorisms that penetrate mind to awaken the heart. The authors have done excellent work in creating a 'meeting of the ways,' showing the place where beloved mystics meet. It is as if they arose from their ancient chambers to uplift our hearts and souls. Ravi Nathwani and Kate Vogt have brought together a collection of remembrance, easy to access, even by using one verse a day. *Mala of the Heart* awakens the heart energy from multiple perspectives, making the poems immortal to our soul."
— Rama Jyoti Vernon, founder of International Yoga College and Center for International Dialogue and cofounder of *Yoga Journal*

"The coeditors have collected a series of deeply inspirational poems that cut right to the heart of the spiritual quest and trigger moments of insight and awakening. A great book to keep with you at all times."
— Lama Tsultrim Allione, author of *Women of Wisdom* and *Feeding Your Demons: Ancient Wisdom for Resolving Inner Conflict*

"The true poet attends to the presentation of truth with an austere language. A single poem has the potential to shift consciousness to make us feel, think, and see differently. Words have neither the power to hide nor reveal truth. Yet, somehow, the poem nourishes the depths of our being since the poem is not limited to language, not limited to words. We deprive ourselves of one of the great assets of life when we fail to read poetry on a frequent basis. It is appropriate that the coeditors have selected 108 poems. That number in the East represents Infinity. A single poem, even a single line, has the potential to awaken us to infinite discoveries. Here you will find a treasure trove of precious poems. Read slowly so a poem enables you to live fully and infinitely rather than as limited creatures with limited sensibilities."

— Christopher Titmuss, author of
Light on Enlightenment and *An Awakened Life*

"The poetry of the mystics past and present leads us into a quietude of heart, the home of the deepest love and wisdom. This wonderful anthology of poetry inspires, enlivens, and brings joy."

— Christina Feldman, cofounder of Gaia House, UK, and author of *Woman Awake* and *Heart of Wisdom, Mind of Calm*

MALA OF THE HEART

108 Sacred Poems

EDITED BY
Ravi Nathwani and Kate Vogt
FOREWORD BY Jack Kornfield

CONTRIBUTING EDITORS, Kat Foley-Saldeña and Soleil Nathwani

New World Library
Novato, California

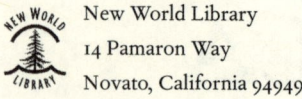 New World Library
14 Pamaron Way
Novato, California 94949

Copyright © 2010 by Ravi Nathwani and Kate Vogt

All rights reserved. This book may not be reproduced in whole or in part, stored in a retrieval system, or transmitted in any form or by any means — electronic, mechanical, or other — without written permission from the publisher, except by a reviewer, who may quote brief passages in a review.

Permission acknowledgments on page 123 are an extension of the copyright page.
Text design by Tona Pearce Myers

Library of Congress Cataloging-in-Publication Data
Mala of the heart : 108 sacred poems / edited by Ravi Nathwani and Kate Vogt ; foreword by Jack Kornfield ; contributing editors, Kat Foley-Saldeña and Soleil Nathwani.
    p.   cm.
ISBN 978-1-57731-677-0 (hardcover : alk. paper)
1. Religious poetry. 2. Mysticism—Poetry. 3. Consolation—Poetry.
I. Nathwani, Ravi. II. Vogt, Kate.
PN6110.R4M3 2010
808.81'9382—dc22   2009033805

First paperback printing, August 2015
ISBN 978-1-60868-378-9
Printed in Canada on 100% postconsumer-waste recycled paper

 New World Library is proud to be a Gold Certified Environmentally Responsible Publisher. Publisher certification awarded by Green Press Initiative. www.greenpressinitiative.org

10 9 8 7 6 5 4 3 2

FOREWORD

YOU HOLD IN YOUR HANDS A WONDERFULLY CRAFTED SET of prayer beads, lovingly fashioned and illuminated in words. Traditionally made of sandalwood, turquoise, amber, or coral, the prayer beads of a *mala* are used to connect the body with the sacred. In the same way, these 108 poems can connect the hearts of each of us who reads them with the sacred understanding of lovers, mystics, and sages across the centuries.

These poems illuminate the true beauty of spiritual practice. Their gift is to open our eyes and hearts to mystery, freedom, and the love that never sleeps. Such poems feed our spirit like music or nectar. In just one line, Lalla of Kashmir gives us pithy instructions for a lifetime: "Meditate within eternity. Don't stay in the mind." She guides us like a child to the breast of our original innocence.

Kabir teaches us how to undertake this as a pilgrimage, to simply sit still until God comes to us. St. Francis places his hands to bless what is beautiful in this world, which is everything. Hafiz advises, "Let love befriend you fully." And Dante assures us that the ascent of the mountain of release becomes milder, "as though you were gliding downstream in a boat." Ah, how sweet the melody of the holy in words.

Read these poems slowly. Savor them. Then, as with a mala of prayer beads, read them again. Let them become familiar to your tongue and your heart, and let their deep wisdom guide you to the love and freedom that is your own true nature. This book carries 108 blessings, to which I add my own.

Blessings,
Jack Kornfield
Spirit Rock Meditation Center
Woodacre, California

EDITORS' INTRODUCTION

THIS COLLECTION CELEBRATES THE HEART. Great spiritual and religious traditions teach our hearts to open and heal. Silent practices of prayer, meditation, and contemplation give rise to an ever-deepening awareness and opening of our hearts. Similarly, poetry written by saints and mystics consoles the heart, helping it to open in a way that is quite unique from that of other art forms. Such poetry represents the resounding silence and brilliance of the infinite "supreme." When we read or listen to poetry of the spirit, we come to see with a certain clarity the one thing that has always been facing us, yet seems invisible to us.

In this poetry, the supreme comes to life through sound, syllable, word, rhythm, and pause. Poetry expresses the peaceful language of the divine heart. An unseen, sacred thread unites our hearts with those of the poets. Like stars in the nighttime sky, a heart that longs to commune with the divine shines alongside the luminous heart of pure being. In a profound moment during the great Sufi poet Rumi's illumined life he noted that "going in search of the heart I found a rose under my feet." So simple was his realization. Throughout years of endless searching, there had been many places and countless roads. Only when the distances disappeared did the search end. That elusive mystery that Rumi sought was there, teasingly, in the form of a rose. Short yet filled with endless wisdom, the poems in this collection are like Rumi's rose, subtle signposts of the most sacred.

The sequencing of the poems is inspired by an ancient map of our spiritual body. There are said to be seven wheels, or energetic centers, called chakras, along our inner spine. Each chakra correlates with a state of consciousness, ranging from day-to-day awareness to pure consciousness and true knowing. In the center of the chest, next to our physical heart, is our heart chakra (*Anāhata-chakra*), where there is an arising and subsiding flow of the unending, energetic life force. The sequence of chakras loosely represents our path of awakening from intense longing to pure understanding of the supreme. At the core of this collection is the illumined heart.

The number of poems is 108. This number symbolizes the divine and sacred connections in our arts, sciences, mathematics, philosophies, and religions. At the highest level, 108 represents the nameless supreme that is beyond worldly existence. Throughout the world, we use a sacred strand of 108 beads, called a rosary or a mala (Sanskrit), for daily meditation and prayer. In our mathematics and sciences, there are numerous references to this auspicious number. For example, 108 is a multiple of the essential numbers 2, 3, and 4 as well as a product of the powers of 1, 2, and 3. Astrologically, the nine planets multiplied by the twelve signs of the sun of the zodiac is 108. The number also represents the relationship between our planetary home, the earth, and the everlasting sun. Hence, a collection of 108 poems is an expression of the ever-present supreme.

Most of the poems are from saints and mystics who lived and died before 1900. Although Rumi appears the most often, with twenty-four poems, there was an effort to have a balanced representation of gender as well as a range of cultures and civilizations. Some of the poems express belief in a higher being and refer to the supreme by name. Some convey instantaneous awakening, while others evoke reverence for a disciplined path of passion, devotion, or contemplation. In contemplative reading of or listening to such poetry, there arises an unending silence that tugs at the soul's aspiration to wisdom, bringing an understanding of what is said between the lines. This can profoundly change our perspective forever.

The philosophical perspective in the selection of the poems echoes the view that the purest connection to our luminous essence is in our hearts. Longing turned inward toward our hearts discovers the hue of the rose, the brightness of the sun, and the mystery of all mysteries. In the light of divine knowledge, our hearts glow with an intense brilliance. Our body, our mind, all of nature, and the entire universe sparkle with pure clarity. The radiant essence is everywhere beyond our words, beyond time, and beyond space, forever present. The light that we could not see welcomes and enfolds us. It floods the thorny landscape of our selves and dissolves the bonds that hold us to our fears. Deep silence arises and fills the eternal vastness of our hearts with wisdom and love.

The truth is that our hearts are the doorway to the immortal stillness and a luminous presence. Common gestures and sayings, such as "The heart knows all" and "Search within your heart," spark remembrance that our thinking mind is the obstacle to the truth. The simple gesture of drawing our hands together over our physiological heart reminds us that the divine is forever present. Also, in unexpected moments we have experienced the divine source. When we fall in love, our hearts overflow with joy and glorious contentment. When tragedy touches our lives, grace may seep in and carry with it auspicious support and life-changing insights.

We hope the poets' hearts will inspire the opening of the reader's heart, whatever the background of the poet or the reader. We also hope that this collection will be one that you treasure forever. Rather than serving as a poetic vacation from worldly life, our wish for you, the reader, is that the reading and rereading of a poem will invite an ever-deepening awareness of your true nature.

If you have a spirit, lose it,
loose it to return where with one word,
we came from.
Now, thousands of words,
and we refuse to leave.

RUMI

Persia (Afghanistan)

Keep walking, though there's no place to get to.
Don't try to see through the distances.
That's not for human beings. Move within,
but don't move the way fear makes you move.

RUMI

Persia (Afghanistan)

If you circumambulated every holy shrine in the world
ten times,
it would not get you to heaven
as quick
as controlling your
anger.

KABIR

India

What is it
you want to change?
Your hair, your face, your body?
Why?
For God is
in love with all those things
and He might weep
when they are
gone.

ST. CATHERINE OF SIENA

Italy

If you want money more than anything,
you'll be bought and sold.
If you have a greed for food,
you'll be a loaf of bread.
This is a subtle truth:
whatever you love, you are.

RUMI

Persia (Afghanistan)

Meditate within eternity.
Don't stay in the mind.
Your thoughts are like a child fretting
near its mother's breast, restless
and afraid, who with a little guidance,
can find the path of courage.

LALLA

India

Life is given.
Nothing is earned,
so learn to serve others,
not your own desire and greed
and ego. They steal your energies,
whereas devotion builds your strength
and protects the intelligent flame
that leads to the truth within.

LALLA

India

Are you jealous of the ocean's generosity?
Why would you refuse to give
this joy to anyone?
Fish don't hold the sacred liquid in cups.
They swim the huge fluid freedom.

RUMI

Persia (Afghanistan)

I know a cure for sadness:
Let your hands touch something that
makes your eyes
smile.

I bet there are a hundred objects close by
that can do that.

Look at
beauty's gift to us —
her power is so great she enlivens
the earth, the sky, our
soul.

MIRABAI

India

When will my shame fall away?
When will I accept being mocked
and let my robe of dignity burn up?

When the wandering pony inside
comes calm to my hand.

LALLA

India

The weight of arrogance is such
that no bird can fly
carrying it.

And the man who feels superior
to others, that man
cannot dance,

the real dance when the soul takes God
into its arms and you both fall
onto your knees in
gratitude,

a blessed gratitude
for life.

ST. JOHN OF THE CROSS

Spain

Complaint
is only possible

while living in the suburbs
of God.

Hafiz

Persia (Iran)

It is your destiny to see as God sees,
to know as God knows,
to feel as God
feels.
How is this possible? How?
Because divine love cannot defy its very self.

Divine love will be eternally true to its own being,
and its being is giving all it can,
at the perfect
moment.

And the greatest gift
God can give is His own experience.

Every object,
every creature, every man, woman and child
has a soul and it is the destiny of all,
to see as God sees, to know as God knows,
to feel as God feels, to Be
as God
Is.

MEISTER ECKHART

Germany

It's the old shell trick with a twist:
I saw God put Himself in one
of your pockets.

You are bound
to find
Him.

※

TUKARAM

India

God
bloomsfrom the shoulder
of the
elephant
who becomes
courteous
to the
ant.

HAFIZ

Persia (Iran)

I felt in need of a great pilgrimage
so I sat still for three
days

and God
came to me.

KABIR

India

I could not lie anymore so I started to call my dog
"God."
First he looked
confused,

then he started smiling, then he even
danced.

I kept at it: now he doesn't even
bite.

I am wondering if this
might work on
people?

TUKARAM

India

What I most want
is to spring out of this personality,
then to sit apart from that leaping.
I've lived too long where I can be reached.

Rumi

Persia (Afghanistan)

God is a pure no-thing,
concealed in now and here:
the less you reach for him,
the more he will appear.

ANGELUS SILESIUS

Bohemia (Poland)

Dear God, please reveal to us
your sublime
beauty

that is everywhere, everywhere, everywhere,

so that we will never again
feel frightened.

My divine love, my love,
please let us touch
your face.

ST. FRANCIS OF ASSISI

Italy

I ask all blessings,
I ask them with reverence,
of my mother earth,
of the sky, moon, and sun my father.

I am old age: the essence of life,
I am the source of all happiness.

All is peaceful, all in beauty,
all in harmony, all in joy.

Anonymous Navajo

Navajo Nation

I cannot dance, O Lord,
unless You lead me.
If You wish me to leap joyfully,
let me see You dance and sing —

Then I will leap into Love —
and from Love into Knowledge,
and from Knowledge into the Harvest,
that sweetest Fruit beyond human sense.

There I will stay with You, whirling.

MECHTILD OF MAGDEBURG

Germany

Love, you have wrecked my body.
Keep doing
that.

I am more well with this deep ache
of missing
you
than content with the
physical wonders
you can pacify
us with.

Mirabai

India

I went everywhere with longing
in my eyes, until here
in my own house

I felt truth
filling my sight.

LALLA

India

How
did the rose
ever open its heart
and give to this world all of its beauty?
It felt the encouragement of light against its being,
otherwise we all remain too
frightened.

HAFIZ

Persia (Iran)

A fish cannot drown in water,
a bird does not fall in air.
In the fire of its making,
Gold doesn't vanish:
The fire brightens.
Each creature God made
must live in its own true nature;
how could I resist my nature,
that lives for oneness with God?

MECHTILD OF MAGDEBURG

Germany

This piece of food cannot be eaten,
nor this bit of wisdom found by looking.
There is a secret core in everyone
not even Gabriel can know by trying to know.

Rumi

Persia (Afghanistan)

What they undertook to do
They brought to pass;
All things hang like a drop of dew
Upon a blade of grass.

W. B. YEATS

Ireland

How
do I
listen to others?
As if everyone were my Master
speaking to me
his
cherished
last
words.

HAFIZ

Persia (Iran)

That one is blessed and at peace
Who doesn't hope, to whom
Desire makes no more loans.

Nothing coming, nothing owned.

※

LALLA

India

I was delighted with myself,
having offered everything I had;
my heart, my faith, my work.

"And who are you," you said,
"to think you have so much to offer?
It seems you have forgotten
where you've come from."

RUMI

Persia (Afghanistan)

Like a great starving beast
my body is quivering
fixed
on the scent
of
Light.

HAFIZ

Persia (Iran)

There is a channel between voice and presence,
a way where information flows.

In disciplined silence the channel opens.
With wandering talk, it closes.

RUMI

Persia (Afghanistan)

Look
what happens to the scale
when love
holds
it.

It
stops
working.

KABIR

India

Knowledge always deceives.

It always limits the Truth, every concept and image does.

From cage to cage the caravan moves,
but I give thanks,

for at each divine juncture
my wings expand
and I

touch Him more
intimately.

MEISTER ECKHART

Germany

Only
that Illumined
One

who keeps
seducing the formless into form
had the charm to win my
heart.

Only a Perfect One
who is always
laughing at the word
two

can make you know
of love.

HAFIZ

Persia (Iran)

True love in every moment praises God.
Longing love brings a sorrow sweet to the pure.
Seeking love belongs to itself alone.
Understanding love gives itself equally to all.
Enlightened love is mingled with the sadness of the world.
But selfless love bears an effortless fruit,
working so quietly even the body cannot say how it comes and goes.

MECHTILD OF MAGDEBURG

Germany

On the way to God the difficulties
feel like being ground by a millstone,
like night coming at noon, like
lightning through the clouds.

But don't worry!
What must come, comes.
Face everything with love,
as your mind dissolves in God.

LALLA

India

God, whose love and joy
are present everywhere,
can't come to visit you
unless you aren't there.

ANGELUS SILESIUS

Bohemia (Poland)

Sometimes afraid of reunion, sometimes
of separation: You and I, so fond of the notion
of a *you* and an *I*, should live
as though we'd never heard those pronouns.

Rumi

Persia (Afghanistan)

Love is
the funeral pyre
where I have laid my living body.

All the false notions of myself
that once caused fear, pain,
have turned to ash
as I neared God.

What has risen
from the tangled web of thought and sinew
now shines with jubilation
through the eyes of angels
and screams from the guts of
Infinite existence
itself.

Love is the funeral pyre
where the heart must lay
its body.

HAFIZ

Persia (Iran)

Ironic, but one of the most intimate acts
of our body is
death.

So beautiful appeared my death — knowing who then I
would kiss,
I died a thousand times before I died.

"Die before you die," said the Prophet
Muhammad.

Have wings that feared ever
touched the Sun?

I was born when all I once
feared — I could
love.

RABIA

Persia (Iraq)

Children
can easily open the drawer

that lets the spirit rise up and wear
its favorite costume of
mirth and laughter.

When the mind is consumed with
remembrance of
Him

something divine happens to the
heart

that
shapes the hand and tongue
and eye into the word
love.

HAFIZ

Persia (Iran)

Love is that that never sleeps,
nor even rests, nor stays
for long with those that do.

Love is language
that cannot be said,
or heard.

RUMI

Persia (Afghanistan)

The way of love is not
a subtle argument.

The door there
is devastation.

Birds make great sky-circles
of their freedom.
How do they learn it?

They fall, and falling,
they're given wings.

RUMI

Persia (Afghanistan)

Drumsound rises on the air,
its throb, my heart.

A voice inside the beat
says, "I know you're tired,
but come. This is the way."

Rumi

Persia (Afghanistan)

O my Lord,
the stars glitter
and the eyes of men are closed.
Kings have locked their doors
and each lover is alone with his love.

Here, I am alone with You.

RABIA

Persia (Iraq)

You're in my eyes.
How else could I see light?

You're in my brain.
This wild joy.

If love did not live in matter,
how would any place have
any hold on anyone?

RUMI

Persia (Afghanistan)

Lord, you are my lover,
my longing,
my flowing stream,
my sun,
and I am your reflection.

Mechtild of Magdeburg

Germany

I live where darkness
is not,
where I am happy.
I am not troubled by coming and going
and am beyond all vision,
above all spheres.
His spirit lives in my soul.
Mukta says: he is my heart's
only home.

MUKTA BAI

India

Wisdom is
sweeter than honey,
brings more joy
than wine,
illumines
more than the sun,
is more precious
than jewels.
She causes
the ears to hear
and the heart to comprehend.

I love her
like a mother,
and she embraces me
as her own child.
I will follow
her footprints
and she will not cast me away.

MAKEDA, QUEEN OF SHEBA

Sheba (Ethiopia/Yemen)

Even
after
all this time
the sun never says to the earth,

"You owe me."
Look what happens
with a love like that —
it lights the whole
world.

HAFIZ

Persia (Iran)

Wherever
God lays His glance
life starts clapping.

The myriad
creatures grab their instruments
and join the song.

Whenever love makes itself known
against another
body.

The
jewel in the eye starts
to
dance.

HAFIZ

Persia (Iran)

Ah, not to be cut off,
not through the slightest partition
shut out from the law of the stars.
The inner — what is it?
if not intensified sky,
hurled through with birds and deep
with the winds of homecoming.

RAINER MARIA RILKE

Bohemia (Czech Republic)

Observe your life, between two breaths.

Breath is a wind, both coming and going.

On this wind you have built your life —
but how will a castle rest on a cloud?

Avicenna

Persia (Uzbekistan)

If you live on the breath,
you won't be tortured
by hunger and thirst,
or the longing to touch.

The purpose of being born is fulfilled
in the state between "I am"
and "That."

LALLA

India

To place You in my heart
may turn You into thought.
I will not do that!
To hold You with my eyes
may turn You into thorn.
I will not do that!
I will set You on my breath
so You will become my life.

RUMI

Persia (Afghanistan)

Know
the true nature of your
Beloved.

In
His
loving eyes
your every thought, word, and movement
is always, always

beautiful.

※

HAFIZ

Persia (Iran)

Cut brambles long enough,
sprout after sprout,
and the lotus will bloom
of its own accord:
Already waiting in the clearing,
the single image of light.
The day you see this,
that day you will become it.

SUN BU-ER

China

Mountains are steadfast but the mountain streams
go by, go by,
and yesterdays are like the rushing streams,
they fly, they fly,
and the great heroes, famous for a day,
they die, they die.

HWANG CHIN-I

Korea

This mountain of release is such that the
ascent's most painful at the start, below;
the more you rise, the milder it will be.
And when the slope feels gentle to the point that
climbing up sheer rock is effortless
as though you were gliding downstream in a boat,
then you will have arrived where this path ends.

<center>~~~</center>

DANTE

Italy

When
the words stop
and you can endure the silence

that reveals your heart's pain
of emptiness
or that great wrenching-sweet longing,

that is the time to try and listen
to what the Beloved's eyes
most want to
say.

HAFIZ

Persia (Iran)

Which is worth more, a crowd of thousands,
or your own genuine solitude?
Freedom, or power over an entire nation?

A little while alone in your room
will prove more valuable than anything else
that could ever be given you.

RUMI

Persia (Afghanistan)

Nothing move thee;
nothing terrify thee;
everything passes;
God never changes.
Patience be all to thee.
Who trusts in God, he
never shall be needy.
God alone suffices.

ST. TERESA OF AVILA

Spain

Sing, my tongue; sing, my hand;
sing, my feet, my knee,
my loins, my
whole body.

Indeed I am His
choir.

ST. THOMAS AQUINAS

Italy

Playfully you hid from me.
All day I looked.

Then I discovered
I was you,

and the celebration
of That began.

LALLA

India

I do not call it his sign,
I do not call it becoming one with his sign.
I do not call it union,
I do not call it harmony with union.
I do not say something has happened,
I do not say nothing has happened.
I will not name it You,
I will not name it I.
Now that the White Jasmine Lord is myself,
what use for words at all?

MAHÂDÊVIYAKKA

India

Although he has no form
my eyes saw him
and his glory shines in my mind,
which knows his secret
inner form
invented by the soul.
What is beyond the mind,
has no boundary.
In it our senses end.
Mukta says: Words cannot contain him,
yet in him all words are.

Mukta Bai

India

There is a desert
I long to be walking,
a wide emptiness,

peace beyond any
understanding of it.

RUMI

Persia (Afghanistan)

The great sea has set me in motion,
set me adrift,
moving me like a weed in a river.

The sky and the strong wind
have moved the spirit inside me
till I am carried away
trembling with joy.

UVAVNUK

Inuit Nation

I am looking for a poem that says Everything
so I don't have to write
anymore.

TUKARAM

India

O friends on this Path,
my eyes are no longer my eyes.
A sweetness has entered through them,
has pierced through to my heart.
For how long did I stand in the house of this body
and stare at the road?
My Beloved is a steeped herb,
he has cured me for life.
Mira belongs to Giridhara, the One who lifts all,
and everyone says she is mad.

MIRABAI

India

We
bloomed in Spring.

Our bodies
are the leaves of God.

The apparent seasons of life and death
our eyes can suffer;

but our souls, dear, I will just say this forthright:
they are God
Himself,

we will never perish
unless He
does.

St. Teresa of Avila

Spain

Out beyond ideas of wrongdoing and rightdoing,
there is a field. I'll meet you there.

When the soul lies down in that grass,
the world is too full to talk about.
Ideas, language, even the phrase *each other*
doesn't make any sense.

❦

Rumi

Persia (Afghanistan)

I have lived on the lip
of insanity, wanting to know reasons,
knocking on a door. It opens.
I've been knocking from the inside!

RUMI

Persia (Afghanistan)

Listen, if you can stand to.
Union with the Friend means not being who you've been,
being instead silence: A place: A view
where language is inside seeing.

RUMI

Persia (Afghanistan)

Between living and dreaming
there is a third thing.
Guess it.

ANTONIO MACHADO

Spain

Birth, old age,
sickness, and death:
From the beginning,
this is the way
things have always been.
Any thought
of release from this life
will wrap you only more tightly
in its snares.
The sleeping person
looks for a Buddha,
the troubled person
turns toward meditation.
But the one who knows
that there's nothing to seek
knows too that there's nothing to say.
She keeps her mouth closed.

DIEU NHAN

Vietnam

He who binds to himself a joy
does the winged life destroy.
But he who kisses the joy as it flies
lives in eternity's sun rise.

WILLIAM BLAKE

England

One instant is eternity;
eternity is the now.
When you see through this one instant,
you see through the one who sees.

WU-MEN

China

I was sad one day and went for a walk;
I sat in a field.

A rabbit noticed my condition and
came near.

It often does not take more than that to help at times —

to just be close to creatures who
are so full of knowing,
so full of love
that they don't
— chat,

they just gaze with
their
marvelous understanding.

ST. JOHN OF THE CROSS

Spain

In my travels I spent time with a great yogi.
Once he said to me,

"Become so still you hear the blood flowing
through your veins."

One night as I sat in quiet,
I seemed on the verge of entering a world inside so vast
I know it is the source of
all of
us.

MIRABAI

India

Tenderly, I now touch all things,

knowing one day we will part.

❧

ST. JOHN OF THE CROSS

Spain

God has never really spoken,
though a thought once crossed His mind.
It is the echo of divine
silence

we hear the birds sing, and that
is the source of all
we see and
touch.

TUKARAM

India

Spring overall. But inside us
there's another unity.

Behind each eye here,
one glowing weather.

Every forest branch moves differently
in the breeze, but as they sway
they connect at the roots.

RUMI

Persia (Afghanistan)

Our hands imbibe like roots,
so I place them on what is beautiful in this world.

And I fold them in prayer, and they
draw from the heavens
light.

ST. FRANCIS OF ASSISI

Italy

We know nothing until we know everything.

I have no object to defend
for all is of equal value
to me.

I cannot lose anything in this
place of abundance
I found.

If something my heart cherishes
is taken away,
I just say, "Lord, what
happened?"

And a hundred more
appear.

―※―

ST. CATHERINE OF SIENA

Italy

I am filled with you.
Skin, blood, bone, brain, and soul.
There's no room for lack of trust, or trust.
Nothing in this existence but that existence.

❦

RUMI

Persia (Afghanistan)

Self inside self, You are nothing but me.
Self inside self, I am only You.

What we are together
will never die.

The why and how of this?
What does it matter?

LALLA

India

I used to have fiery intensity,
and a flowing sweetness.

The waters were illusion.
The flames, made of snow.

Was I dreaming then?
Am I awake now?

RUMI

Persia (Afghanistan)

I know how it will be when I die,
my beauty will be so extraordinary that God
will worship me.
He will not worship me from a distance, for our minds
will have wed,
our souls will have flowed into each other.
How to say this: God and I
will forever cherish
Myself.

RABIA

Persia (Iraq)

I searched for my Self
until I grew weary,

but no one, I know now,
reaches the hidden knowledge
by means of effort.

Then, absorbed in "Thou art This,"
I found the place of Wine.

There all the jars are filled,
but no one is left to drink.

LALLA

India

Being is not what it seems,
nor non-being. The world's
existence is not
in the world.

RUMI

Persia (Afghanistan)

I think God might be a little prejudiced.
For once He asked me to join Him on a walk
through this world,

and we gazed into every heart on this earth,
and I noticed He lingered a bit longer
before any face that was weeping,
and before any eyes that were laughing.

And sometimes when we passed
a soul in worship
God too would kneel down.

I have come to learn: God
adores His creation.

ST. FRANCIS OF ASSISI

Italy

If God
invited you to a party and
said,

"Everyone in the ballroom tonight will
be my special
guest,"

how would you then treat them when you arrived?

Indeed, indeed!

And Hafiz knows that there is no one in
this world who is not standing upon

His jeweled dance
floor.

HAFIZ

Persia (Iran)

All day and night, music,
a quiet, bright
reedsong. If it
fades, we fade.

RUMI

Persia (Afghanistan)

The love of God, unutterable and perfect,
flows into a pure soul the way that light
rushes into a transparent object.
The more love that it finds, the more it gives
itself; so that, as we grow clear and open,
the more complete the joy of heaven is.
And the more souls who resonate together,
the greater the intensity of their love,
and, mirror-like, each soul reflects the other.

DANTE

Italy

When the body becomes Your mirror,
how can it serve?

When the mind becomes Your mind,
what is left to remember?

Once my life is Your gesture,
how can I pray?

When all my awareness is Yours,
what can there be to know?

I became You, Lord, and forgot You.

MAHÂDÊVIYAKKA

India

To learn the scriptures is easy,
to live them, hard.
The search for the Real
is no simple matter.

Deep in my looking,
the last words vanished.
Joyous and silent,
the waking that met me there.

LALLA

India

Alleluia! light
burst from your untouched
womb like a flower
on the farther side
of death. The world-tree
is blossoming. Two
realms become one.

HILDEGARD OF BINGEN

Germany
Translated by Barbara Newman

u
n
i
v
e
r
s
e

?
?
?

Tukaram

India

Who speaks the sound of an echo?
Who paints the image in a mirror?
Where are the spectacles in a dream?
Nowhere at all — that's the nature of mind!

Tree-Leaf Woman

India

God

dissolved

my mind — my separation.

I cannot describe now my intimacy with Him.

How dependent is your body's life on water and food and air?

I said to God, "I will always be unless you cease to Be,"

and my Beloved replied, "And I

would cease to Be

if you

died."

ST. TERESA OF AVILA

Spain

Die while you're alive
and be absolutely dead.
Then do whatever you want:
it's all good.

Bunan

Japan

Center of all centers, core of cores,
almond self-enclosed and growing sweet —
all this universe, to the furthest stars
and beyond them, is your flesh, your fruit.

Now you feel how nothing clings to you;
your vast shell reaches into endless space,
and there the rich, thick fluids rise and flow.
Illuminated in your infinite peace,

a billion stars go spinning through the night,
blazing high above your head.
But in you is the presence that
will be, when all the stars are dead.

RAINER MARIA RILKE
Bohemia (Czech Republic)

Quiet yourself.
Reach out with your mind's skillful hand.
Let it go inside of me
and touch
God.

Don't
be shy, dear.
Every aspect of Light we are meant
to know.

The calm hand holds more
than baskets of goods
from the market.

The calm soul knows more
than anything this world
can offer from her
beautiful
womb.

ST. JOHN OF THE CROSS

Spain

To see a World in a Grain of Sand
and a Heaven in a Wild Flower,
Hold Infinity in the palm of your hand
and Eternity in an hour.

WILLIAM BLAKE

England

Om
Shanti, Shanti, Shanti
Om

POETS

ANONYMOUS NAVAJO (19th–20th century, Navajo Nation)

AVICENNA (Abū Alī Sīnā, Ibn Sīnā) (980–1037, Persia [Uzbekistan]) was born into a middle-class family near Bukhara, in present-day Uzbekistan. By age eighteen he had memorized the Qur'an and a great deal of Persian poetry, and he had achieved status as a physician. Avicenna is one the foremost Islamic philosophers and authored almost 450 books on philosophy, medicine, theology, geometry, astronomy, and the like. In the West, Avicenna is well known for fathering modern medicine and influencing Christian philosophers. His poems are written in Persian and Arabic and include one that describes the descent of the soul into the body from the Higher Sphere.

WILLIAM BLAKE (1757–1827, England) was born in London, where he spent most of his life. In his early years, Blake experienced visions of angels, the Virgin Mary, and historical figures. The memories of these visions are said to have influenced him throughout his life. Blake began writing poetry at the age of twelve, and he apprenticed as an engraver before setting out on his life as a poet, painter, visionary mystic, and engraver. Blake challenged the values and views of his time and was widely misunderstood. Some considered him a madman. After his death, critics came to regard Blake as a genius for his expressiveness and creativity and for the mystical undercurrents within his work.

BUNAN (Shido Bunan) (1603–1676, Japan) Zen Master.

ST. CATHERINE OF SIENA (1347–1380, Italy) was born the youngest of twenty or more children to a wool dyer. It is said that at age six she was transformed by a vision of Jesus and three of his apostles. In her teens Catherine resisted the pressure to marry and became a Dominican nun. She was an ardent mystic and great Catholic saint who dictated her ideas on spirituality and devotion in what became known as her *Letters*. Catherine selflessly served the poor and eased the suffering of those who sought her counsel. In 1970, Pope Paul VI proclaimed St. Catherine a "Doctor of the Church."

DANTE (Dante Alighieri) (1265–1321, Italy) was born into a prominent family in Florence. In 1290, after the death of the woman he loved, Dante plunged into intense study of classical philosophy and Provençal poetry. This woman is thought to have been Beatrice Portinari, Dante's acknowledged source of spiritual inspiration. Dante is best known as the author of the long poem *Commedia* (the adjective *Divina* was added in the 1600s). Unlike many of his contemporaries, Dante viewed man's twofold duty as realizing both earthly happiness and everlasting life. He considered the individual soul as part of a collective whole.

DIEU NHAN (Ly Ngoc Kieu) (1041–1113, Vietnam) was a daughter of a prince, a goddaughter of a king, and married to a district chief. After her husband passed away, she became a Buddhist and studied with a Zen master; she later became head of the seventeenth generation of the Vinitaruci school. Zen master Dieu Nhan served as director of the Huong Hai temple and was recognized as one of the two most distinguished woman poets of her time.

MEISTER ECKHART (Johannes Eckhart) (1260–1328, Germany) was born in Germany and entered the Dominican order as a young man. As an eminent public figure, he was popular for his powerful and beautiful style of expressing his contemplative experiences. Like other great mystics, Eckhart used metaphors to express what lies beyond words. His poetry often communicates the importance of silence. Eckhart's popularity protected him from accusations of heresy, but after his death many of his works were suppressed for several centuries. Since 1980, the Dominican order has taken steps to reveal Meister Eckhart as a great Christian mystic.

ST. FRANCIS OF ASSISI (1182–1226, Italy) was born into a wealthy merchant family. Experiences of illness and service in the military caused him to question the purpose of life. It is said that, one day when Francis was in church, God's voice awakened him to a spiritual path. Francis renounced his father's wealth and devoted himself to a life of poverty in service to the poor. He founded the Order of the Friars Minor, who take no property and express intense love for God through word and action. Francis was so passionately devoted to God that he would wildly sing and dance his praise. Known as the patron saint of the animals and the environment, Francis created hymns and teachings that proclaimed both the ability and duty to protect and enjoy nature.

HAFIZ (Khwāja Šams ud-Dīn Muḥammad Hāfez-e Šīrāzī) (ca. 1320–1389, Persia [Iran]) was born in the garden city of Shiraz. It is said that after the early death of his father, Hafiz worked for a bakery, where he caught sight of Shakh-e Nabat, whose incredible beauty moved him to write and sing of his love for her. During a forty-night vigil to win this girl's love, Hafiz had a vision of an angel, whose beauty led Hafiz to realize that God was infinitely more beautiful than any human form. The angel revealed where Hafiz could find a spiritual master. Hafiz then met and became a disciple of Attar of Shiraz, who led Hafiz to union with God. Like other great Sufi poets, Hafiz employed imagery to express his longing and love for the divine.

HILDEGARD OF BINGEN (1098–1179, Germany) was born the tenth child of a noble family, and as was customary with the tenth child, she was dedicated at birth to the church.

From an early age, Hildegard had luminous visions, yet she kept this gift concealed from all except her teacher and secretary. When she was forty-two, a vision of God commanded her to write down everything she observed in her visions. Although Hildegard never doubted the origin of her visions, she successfully sought to have them sanctioned by the Catholic Church. Hildegard gained fame as a remarkable mystic throughout Europe for her theological, botanical, and medicinal texts, as well as for her letters, music, and poems.

HWANG CHIN-I (1506–1544, Korea) lived in Songdo and was famous during the reign of King Chungjong. Though a certain mystique surrounds her life, Chin-i's poetic legacy of linking word and image has elevated her to cultural icon in Korea. Chin-i was a *kisaeng*-singer-poet. A few of her poems on love and freedom are celebrated even today. Whether or not the poems were intended solely as expressions of human desire, they capture the imagination of spiritual seekers.

ST. JOHN OF THE CROSS (1542–1591, Spain) was born Juan de Yepes y Alvarez; his family had been Jewish but were *conversos* ("forced Christians"). John worked in many trades and received his first formal education at a Jesuit school. At age twenty-one, he became a Carmelite friar. Four years later, he met Teresa of Avila, and their joint reform work led to his being imprisoned and tortured for nine months by his fellow priests. While in prison, John had a life-transforming realization of the veil that separates us from God. His axiom was that the soul must empty itself of self in order to be filled with God. After escaping from prison, he lived a life of joyful solitude.

KABIR (Kabir Das) (ca. 1440–1518, India) was raised by a Muslim family of weavers, though legend has it that his birth mother may have been a Brahmin widow. Kabir became a disciple of the Hindu bhakti saint Ramananda at an early age, and his name is often interpreted as "Guru's Grace." Though a great mystic and a contemplative, Kabir never abandoned worldly life. He sought to bridge the religious cultures yet was denounced by mainstream religious leaders during his lifetime. At Kabir's death, his body turned to flowers, and his Hindu and Muslim followers each took half to perform last rites. A saint in the bhakti and Sufi tradition, Kabir expressed through his poetry self-surrender, divine love, and inward worship of the beloved with the heart.

LALLA (Lal Diddi, Laleswari, Lal Ded) (est. 14th c.) was born in Kashmir in northern India. She was married at the age of twelve, and after years of harsh treatment at the hands of her mother-in-law and her husband, she left to live the life of a wandering devotee in the Shaivite tradition. Renouncing the world, Lalla expressed her joyful union with her beloved Lord through song and dance. The realizations of this great saint and mystic appeal to the hearts of people across cultural and religious barriers.

ANTONIO MACHADO (1875–1939, Spain) was born in Seville but emigrated to Paris, where he worked as a translator and met great French poets. At age thirty-four Machado married, although his beloved Leonor died after only a few years of marriage. Distraught over the loss of his wife, Machado manifested a sacred spiritual yearning in his work, echoing the divine experience of mystics several centuries earlier. Machado is considered one of Spain's most popular playwrights and poets.

MAHÂDÊVIYAKKA (Akka Mahadevi) (12th century, India) was born in the Indian village of Udatadi and initiated into the worship of Lord Shiva at age ten. Though a local ruler fell in love with her and they married, Mahâdêviyakka left him to live the life of a wandering Shiva devotee. She is known for her passionate devotional (bhakti) poetry, always written to the "Lord white as jasmine." It is said that Mahâdêviyakka died in her twenties, having reached oneness with her mystical husband Shiva at Srisaila, the Holy Mountain.

MAKEDA (queen of Sheba, Bilqis) (ca. 1000 BCE, Sheba [Ethiopia]). There are few verifiable details on Makeda's life, although she figures prominently in Judaic, Islamic, and Ethiopian traditions. There are many accounts of her journey to ancient Israel to meet King Solomon in search of wisdom. This legendary voyage has inspired centuries of speculation about her kingdom and influence in the ancient world. Makeda is said to have been renowned for her beauty, purity, and love for wisdom.

MECHTILD OF MAGDEBURG (ca. 1207–1282, Germany) was born into a wealthy family and at age twelve said that she saw "all things in God, and God in all things." In her early twenties, she entered the Beguines sisterhood and led a life of simplicity, service, and prayer. Over a fourteen-year period, she received ongoing mystical visions and the divine instruction to record these experiences. Mechtild's love poetry has been compared to that of the Sufi poets of the Middle East and the bhakti poets of India.

MIRABAI (Mira) (ca. 1498–1565, India) was born into a noble family in northern India. From an early age, she worshipped Krishna. During her marriage to a prominent crown prince, her husband's family actively sought to stop Mirabai's meditations and prayers to Krishna. Upon her husband's death, she refused to throw herself on his funeral pyre, proclaiming that she was wedded to Krishna. Mirabai became a wandering ascetic devoted to Giridhara, a manifestation of Krishna.

MUKTA BAI (13th century, India). It is said that Mukta Bai's father's guru instructed him to leave the life of an ascestic and return to his worldly duty as a householder. Mukta Bai's mother and father had four children together, and the family was spurned by the orthodox authorities because of the father's actions. Both her mother and father died when Mukta Bai was a young girl, and she had to beg to survive. It is said that these early experiences fostered a great spiritual depth in this poet-saint.

RABIA (Sufi Rabi'a, Rabia al Basri) (717–801, Persia [Iraq]) was born into poverty and is said to have been taken by robbers and sold into slavery after her parents died. She endured years of hard work and abuse and spent her nights in prayer and meditation. According to legend, her master freed her when he observed her shrouded in a divine light during her devotions. Once free, Rabia went to the desert, where she became an ascetic. Unlike with other great saints and mystics, her teacher was God himself rather than a master. Rabia introduced the concept that God should be loved for God's own sake, not out of fear.

RAINER MARIA RILKE (1875–1926, Bohemia [Czech Republic]) was born in Prague. Although poetically and artistically gifted, Rilke was sent to a military academy, which he eventually left to study philosophy, art history, and literature. His first poetry was published when he was nineteen, and he became one of the greatest German-language poets. Rilke's lyrical poetry reveals his belief in the coexistence of the material and spiritual realms.

RUMI (Jalāludin Muḥammad Rumi) (1207–1273, Persia [Afghanistan]) was born in Balkh on the eastern edge of the Persian Empire and at age eight settled in Turkey with his family, where Rumi eventually succeeded his father as head of a dervish school. At age thirty-seven Rumi met the whirling dervish Shams-e Tabrīzī, whose divine presence awakened Rumi's own love for the divine. Rumi thus abandoned his scholarly position and began writing poetry, using metaphors to express his experience of mystical union and his intense longing and search for the divine. Rumi reached across cultural and social boundaries, and it is said that his funeral was attended by Persians, Muslims, Jews, Christians, and Greeks.

ANGELUS SILESIUS (Johannes Scheffler) (1624–1677, Bohemia [Poland]) was born into a Polish Lutheran family in Breslau. Due to the influence of the Hapsburgs, Silesius converted to Catholicism as a young adult and was later ordained a Catholic priest. He was drawn to the monastic life because of his own spiritual yearnings. Silesius maintained that God and man are essentially one and longed for union with the divine as Christ.

SUN BU-ER (Sun Pu-erb) (1124–ca. 1182, China) was married and had three children before devoting her life to Daoist practices around age fifty. Her husband had been studying with the Daoist master Wang Chongyang (Wang Ze) for years before Sun Bu-er too became his student. After also becoming a teacher, Sun Bu-er wrote her Daoist teachings in the form of verse for her followers. Full of vivid imagery, her writings impart her own visionary experiences, in which she received teachings from ancient Daoist masters. After Sun Bu-er's death, she was named one of a group of female Daoist masters collectively referred to as the "Seven Immortals."

ST. TERESA OF AVILA (1515–1582, Spain) was born into a noble family. Early in life, Teresa was drawn to prayer and caring for the poor. Her mother died when Teresa was young, and at age sixteen, she transferred to a convent school, where she decided to join the Carmelite order. During periods of severe physical pain caused by an illness, Teresa began to find serene inner peace and experience ecstatic visions. Initially encouraged to abandon these experiences because they were interpreted as demonic, Teresa later was encouraged by a priest to return to her prayers. As one of the great Christian mystics, she became completely absorbed in and devoted to God. At age forty-three, Teresa founded a new order on the vows of poverty and simplicity. She emphasized the importance of experiencing God's love. In 1622, St. Teresa was canonized by the Catholic Church.

ST. THOMAS AQUINAS (1225–1274, Italy) was born into an aristocratic family, and at age five was sent to the Benedictine abbey of Monte Cassino. There he developed a reverent love for the scriptures, contemplation, solitude, and virtue. At age seventeen, Thomas entered the Dominican order. In his early thirties, he was appointed to teach at the University of Paris, where he studied the suppressed Aristotelian texts on metaphysics. Though known for his highly analytical and methodical works, Thomas also experienced periods of mystical ecstasy. He came to know all in creation as revelations of the infinite God.

TREE-LEAF WOMAN (est. 8th–11th century, India) was a practitioner of the Tantric Buddhist tradition in India. In this tradition, upon coming into a state of awakening the practitioner would speak or sing of his or her experience. The songs of Tree-Leaf Woman were recorded by other practitioners present at the time. Her songs express a pure understanding of the nature of the awakened mind and the source of the phenomenal world.

TUKARAM (1608–1649, India) was born in a small village in western India to a family that sold produce. When he was thirteen, both his parents died, leaving him responsible for supporting his remaining family. Years later, after losing his first wife and children to famine, Tukaram retreated within and began to receive visits from Krishna. In the dream state he also received instructions to write divine poetry. His writings led to persecution by Brahmin priests and pundits. Tukaram became increasingly God absorbed, retreating to caves in the hills near his village and singing and dancing in the streets. He is said to have walked off alone one day, never to be seen again.

UVAVNUK (19th–20th century, Inuit Nation) was a Netsilik Inuit shaman. She is said to have gained her shamanic power when struck by a ball of fire that fell from the sky. Knocked senseless, Uvavnuk found herself imbued with a great power when she revived, which she then dedicated to serving her people.

W. B. YEATS (William Butler Yeats) (1865–1939, Ireland) was born in Dublin and received his education in London and Dublin. He had a penchant for mysticism, occultism, and astrology and was influenced by the writings of Emanuel Swedenborg and Hinduism. At the age of twenty-seven, Yeats wrote, "The mystical life is the center of all that I do and all that I think about and all that I write."

WU-MEN (Wu-men Hui-k'ai; Mumom) (1183–1260, China) was a head monk at the Lung-hsiang monastery in China. While at this monastery, Wu-Men assembled *Gateless Gate*, the classic collection of forty-eight koans, which are paradoxical utterances used in Zen meditation as a center of concentration.

SOURCES AND PERMISSION ACKNOWLEDGMENTS

Every effort has been made to trace copyright holders of poetry in this book. The editors apologize if any poetry or other material has been included without permission.

Gratitude is due to the following for permission to include poems or extracts from poetry in copyright.

"If you want money more than anything," "Are you jealous of the ocean's generosity?," "Love is that that never sleeps," "The way of love is not a subtle argument," "Drumsound rises on the air," "You're in my eyes," "Which is worth more, a crowd of thousands," "There is a desert," "Spring overall," and "I used to have fiery intensity": From the MAYPOP publication *Birdsong*, copyright 1993, Rumi, translated by Coleman Barks, and used with his permission.

"Between living and dreaming": From the Wesleyan University Press publication *Times Alone: Selected Poems of Antonio Machado*, copyright 1983, Robert Bly, and used with his permission.

"Out beyond ideas": From the HarperOne publication *The Essential Rumi*, copyright 1997, Rumi, translated by Coleman Barks, and used with his permission.

"Observe your life, between two breaths": From the publication *Love's Alchemy*, copyright 2006, David and Sabrineh Fideler, used by permission of New World Library, Novato, California.

"The weight of arrogance is such," "God blooms from the shoulder," "How do I listen to others?," "Like a great starving beast," "Only that Illumined One," "Complaint," "Love is the funeral pyre," "Children can easily open the drawer," "Wherever God lays His glance," and "When the words stop,": From the Penguin publication *The Gift, Poems by Hafiz*, copyright 1999, Daniel Ladinsky, and used with his permission.

"If you circumambulated every holy shrine in the world," "What is it you want to change?," "I know a cure for sadness," "It is your destiny to see as God sees," "It's the old shell trick with a twist," "I felt in need of a great pilgrimage," "I could not lie anymore so I started to call my dog "God," "Dear God, please reveal to us," "Love, you have wrecked my body," "How did the rose," "Look what happens to the scale," "Knowledge always deceives," "Ironic, but one of the most intimate acts," "Even after all this time," "Know the true nature of your Beloved," "Sing, my tongue," "I was sad one day," "We bloomed," "I am looking for a poem that says Everything," "In my travels I spent time with a great yogi," "God has never really spoken," "Our hands imbibe like roots," "We know nothing until we know everything," "I know how it will be when I die," "I think God might be a little prejudiced," "If God invited you to a party," "Universe," "God Dissolved my mind," "Tenderly," and "Quiet yourself": From the Penguin anthology *Love Poems from God*, copyright 2002, Daniel Ladinsky, and used with his permission.

"God is a pure no-thing," "I ask all blessings," "He who binds to himself," "To see the world," "God, whose love and joy," "Ah, not to be cut off," "This mountain of release is such," "The great sea has set me in motion," "One instant is eternity," "The love of God,

Sources and Permission Acknowledgments

unutterable and perfect," and "Die while you're alive,": From the publication *The Enlightened Heart*, copyright 1989, Stephen Mitchell, reprinted by permission of HarperCollins Publishers, New York, NY.

"If you have a spirit, lose it," "Keep walking, though there's no place to get to," "What I most want," "This piece of food cannot be eaten," "There is a channel between voice and presence," "Sometimes afraid of reunion," "Listen, if you can stand to," "I have lived on the lip," "I am filled with you," "Being is not what it seems," and "All day and night, music": From the publication *Unseen Rain: Quatrains of Rumi*, copyright 1986, John Moyne and Coleman Barks, used by permission of Threshold Books, Putney, VT.

"Alleluia!": From the Cornell University Press publication *Symphonia: A Critical Edition of the Symphonia Armonie Celestium Revelationum*, copyright 1998, author Hildegard of Bingen, translated by Barbara Newman, used by permission of Cornell University Press, Ithaca, NY.

"I was delighted with myself" and "To place you in my heart": From the Thorsons publication *Whispers of the Beloved*, copyright 1999, Rumi, translated by Maryam Mafe and Azima Melia Kolin, reprinted by permission of HarperCollins Publishers Ltd.

"(Buddha in Glory) Center of all centers, core of cores": From the publication *The Selected Poetry of Rainer Maria Rilke*, copyright 1982, Rainer Maria Rilke, translated by Stephen Mitchell, used by permission of Random House, Inc.

"Nothing move thee": From the publication *The Collected Poems of Yvor Winters*, copyright 1978, translated by Yvor Winters, reprinted with permission of www.ohioswallow.com, Swallow Press/Ohio University Press, Athens, Ohio.

"Birth, old age," "Oh my Lord," "O friends on this path," and "When the body becomes": From the publication *Women in Praise of the Sacred*, copyright 1994, Jane Hirshfield, reprinted by permission of HarperCollins Publishers, New York, NY.

"Who speaks the sound of an echo?": From the publication *Passionate Enlightenment*, copyright 1994, Miranda Shaw, reprinted by permission of Princeton University Press, Princeton, NJ.

"Meditate within eternity," "Life is given," "When will my shame fall away?" "That one is blessed and at peace," "If you live on the breath," "I went everywhere with longing," On the way to God the difficulties," "Playfully you hid from me," and "Self inside self": From the MAYPOP publication *Naked Song*, Lalla, copyright 1992, translated by Coleman Barks and reprinted with his permission.

"What they undertook to do": From the Scribner Book Company publication *The Collected Poems of W. B. Yeats*, copyright 1996, William Butler Yeats and editor Richard J. Finneran, reprinted by permission of Simon & Schuster, Inc., New York, NY, and A. P. Watt Ltd, UK.

"Lord": From *Beguine Spirituality*, copyright 1989, Fiona Bowie, translated by Oliver Davies, Crossroad Publishing Company, Danvers, MA.

"Go by, go by": From *Poems from Korea: From the Earliest Era to the Present*, compiled and translated by Peter H. Lee.

"Cut brambles long enough": From *Immortal Sisters: Secret Teachings of Taoist Women*, translated and edited by Thomas Cleary.

"I live where darkness": From *Book of Women Poets: From Antiquity to Now*, edited by Aliki Barnstone.

"Wisdom is sweeter than honey": From *The Queen of Sheba & Her Only Son Menyelek*, translated by E. A. Wallis Budge.

ACKNOWLEDGMENTS

Numerous people have contributed directly or indirectly to this book. The editors especially want to express gratitude to the contributing editors Kat Foley-Saldeña and Soleil Nathwani as well as Jay Rosner for their loving support and involvement in the selection and editing of the collection. We thank Lisa Fitzpatrick for her personal and professional guidance.

POET INDEX

Anonymous Navajo, 21
Avicenna, 55
Blake, William, 79, 107
Bunan, 104
Catherine of Siena, Saint, 4, 87
Dante, 61, 97
Dieu Nhan, 78
Meister Eckhart, 13, 35
Francis of Assisi, Saint, 20, 86, 94
Hafiz, 12, 15, 25, 29, 32, 36, 41, 43, 52, 53, 58, 62, 95
Hildegard of Bingen, 100
Hwang Chin-i, 60
John of the Cross, Saint, 11, 81, 83, 106
Kabir, 3, 16, 34
Lalla, 6, 7, 10, 24, 30, 38, 56, 66, 89, 92, 99
Machado, Antonio, 77
Mahâdêviyakka, 67, 98

Makeda, queen of Sheba, 51
Mechtild of Magdeburg, 22, 26, 37, 49
Mirabai, 9, 23, 72, 82
Mukta Bai, 50, 68
Rabia, 42, 47, 91
Rilke, Rainer Maria, 54, 105
Rumi, 1, 2, 5, 8, 18, 27, 31, 33, 40, 44, 45, 46, 48, 57, 63, 69, 74, 75, 76, 85, 88, 90, 93, 96
Silesius, Angelus, 19, 39
Sun Bu-er, 59
Teresa of Avila, Saint, 64, 73, 103
Thomas Aquinas, Saint, 65
Tree-Leaf Woman, 102
Tukaram, 14, 17, 71, 84, 101
Uvavnuk, 70
Wu-Men, 80
Yeats, W. B., 28

ABOUT THE EDITORS

RAVI NATHWANI was born into a business family in East Africa and raised in India in the Vaishnav Hindu tradition, in which Hindu rituals were integrated into daily life from a very young age. He has become a modern-day messenger of a variety of Vedic studies through his lectures and workshops. Since 1998, Ravi has been teaching at Tufts University. He also teaches Wisdom Yoga and Buddhist meditation at JFK University in California. In the Bay Area, Ravi leads satsangs and meditation groups and teaches the Yoga Sutras of Patanjali and the Bhagavad Gita in Yoga teacher trainings. Ravi has an MBA from Boston University and has lived in Bombay, Boston, and London.

KATE VOGT grew up on a farm in western Kansas. Having lived in Luleå, Frankfurt/Main, Copenhagen, Seattle, New York, and San Francisco, Kate gained fluency in other cultures and languages. She has been a management consultant to universities, museums, and botanical gardens. Her lifelong interest in Yoga has led to study in India with A.G. and Indra Mohan and in the United States with Georg Feuerstein. Kate teaches both classical Yoga and Yoga philosophy privately in San Francisco and Marin County and serves as an instructor of Yoga philosophy at the College of Marin Extension. She has a BA in art history from the University of Washington and an MBA from Seattle University. Kate is a founding advisor of the international Green Yoga Association.

NEW WORLD LIBRARY is dedicated to publishing books and other media that inspire and challenge us to improve the quality of our lives and the world.

We are a socially and environmentally aware company, and we strive to embody the ideals presented in our publications. We recognize that we have an ethical responsibility to our customers, our staff members, and our planet.

We serve our customers by creating the finest publications possible on personal growth, creativity, spirituality, wellness, and other areas of emerging importance. We serve New World Library employees with generous benefits, significant profit sharing, and constant encouragement to pursue their most expansive dreams.

As a member of the Green Press Initiative, we print an increasing number of books with soy-based ink on 100 percent postconsumer-waste recycled paper. Also, we power our offices with solar energy and contribute to nonprofit organizations working to make the world a better place for us all.

Our products are available
in bookstores everywhere.
For our catalog, please contact:

New World Library
14 Pamaron Way
Novato, California 94949

Phone: 415-884-2100 or 800-972-6657
Catalog requests: Ext. 50
Orders: Ext. 52
Fax: 415-884-2199
Email: escort@newworldlibrary.com

To subscribe to our electronic newsletter, visit
www.newworldlibrary.com